Let Me Save You

Let Me Save You

POETIC BIBLE TRUTHS ABOUT JESUS CHRIST

⬦

ERIC ZACK

RESOURCE *Publications* • Eugene, Oregon

LET ME SAVE YOU
Poetic Bible Truths about Jesus Christ

Resource Publications
An Imprint of Wipf and Stock Publishers
199 W. 8th Ave., Suite 3
Eugene, OR 97401

www.wipfandstock.com

PAPERBACK ISBN: 979-8-3852-3349-6
HARDCOVER ISBN: 979-8-3852-3350-2
EBOOK ISBN: 979-8-3852-3351-9

11/19/24

Contents

CONTENTS

Preface

Welcome to my private collection of Christian poetry spanning five total volumes and 173 original, unique poems that I have written over the past thirty years of my life. Each volume deals with key aspects of Christianity and Holy Bible truths that have been revealed to me during my personal struggles. I have organized each one of these into an easy-to-read-and-follow format. Certain lines and stanzas in each of these poems will also have specific Bible verses referenced if you prefer to investigate further, meditate, or dive deeper into the Word.

Volume 1 focuses on God, the Bible, and surrendering. Volume 2 describes Jesus Christ and the need to be born again. Volume 3 highlights important Christian tenants that support living life to its fullest, such as grace, faith, choice, prayer, life, and blessings. Volume 4 depicts evil such as rebellion, pride, Satan, disease, death, and hell. And finally, volume 5 completes my collection with living for the future by applying Christian beliefs and putting this lifestyle into practice in serving others. It covers topics such as the Church, correction, redemption, finding purpose, the rapture, heaven, and the end of times.

I have generally written these poems whenever I had ideas or inspirations come to me and when I had the time to process them, sit down, and compose them (preferably in an uninterrupted manner). Although their actual chronological order has been lost, I feel that there is great benefit in how these poems have been organized for your understanding and reading pleasure. My brain seems to work in this manner by compartmentalizing related topics together. My intention was to document many of my own personal experiences along with my spiritual growth journey, not that I am anyone special in that respect. I'm just an ordinary person whose life experiences have opened my eyes to Jesus at an early point in my young adult life due to certain circumstances. I am so grateful for what has happened in my life and that I was chosen worthy by Jesus to suffer through extreme emotional pain. This has directly led me towards Him. My mom's death was absolutely the worst thing that has ever happened to me; yet in retrospect, it was absolutely the best thing that has ever happened to me. This stark dichotomy remains quite perplexing to me. But I have always wanted to learn what the truth is.

My typical poetry style is to tell an impactful story with powerful emotional details that describe a specific defined topic; and most of them possess some rhythm and rhyming pattern based on the melodies of contemporary music. My hope is that they inspire and speak to you and specifically the younger generation—who might appreciate this form of expression. Most of my poems have been adapted as such, changing the lyrics of these songs to reveal important Bible truths. These melodies are also referenced next to my poem titles. But all of these poems are stand-alone, in that without the melody, they should still make perfect sense. Most of my poems are nonfictional (based on real-life experiences as either being autobiographical or biographical in context); while some are completely fictional (made-up to highlight a particular truth). None of these types really matter in order to highlight the main theme of each poem, nor have these been revealed. One secret I have learned over the years about growing closer to Christ is found in Rom 10:17: "So then faith *comes* by hearing, and hearing by the word of God" (NKJV, italics original). This can be accomplished in many ways and whichever ways you choose; these are pleasing to Him.

I considered my life pretty normal growing up until my mom's death. Then seemingly overnight, my world fell apart, and I felt lost and confused. I didn't know what was happening to me. I asked typical questions like, Why me? and, Why now?, but nothing was revealed to me. Shortly thereafter, my stepfather struggled with alcoholism as a way to self-medicate and numb the emotional pain that he was feeling. And the four of us kids were left to fend for ourselves for our own survival.

I returned to college but barely passed the remaining semesters of my first degree. Nothing as serious as this has ever occurred to me before or ever since thankfully. I was surviving one day at a time and learning valuable lessons as I went through the grieving process internally and privately. It was a slow process for me, as I was still learning who I was, developing into who I wanted to become, all while being a young teenager at heart. All of a sudden, I had to grow up and do so really fast . . . and on my own. Poetry was the only thing that worked for me. Back then, no one had cell phones, and the internet was just created a few years prior to this. Moreover, all of my childhood friends were back in my hometown or away at another college. None of my new college acquaintances could understand what I was going through. Indeed, I felt all alone. Poetry was my only outlet. Putting my emotions down on paper seemed to give these abstract things actual weight, relevance, and true acknowledgment. It also allowed me to literally (physically) and figuratively (emotionally) store my emotions away—as if to feel them, deal with them, learn from them, and then move on from them.

My original intention was simply to try to heal myself—deep down knowing that if I continued to bottle up these emotions over time, I would eventually explode just like a boiling pot of water in a kettle on the stovetop. Introverts need time, privacy, and quiet to process difficult experiences. I did not trust anyone enough to share these vulnerabilities with—for fear of judgment, criticism, or simply being dismissed. I never thought my poems would ultimately be worthy of sharing with others to help them in some way. In the midst of tragedy, you can only think of yourself. However, once you pass through that tragedy, you eventually regain a sense of others in the world and can see life and future possibilities and new opportunities more clearly. My hope and prayers are that my poems can help some of you in whatever you are facing today, whether it be serious or trivial, permanent or temporary, or spiritual, psychosocial, and/or physical. I now realize that Jesus was the only one who could heal me and not as a result of my own efforts. My efforts only proved to be futile attempts to try to do what only God can do. I have learned this valuable lesson to let go of certain things that I cannot control.

I have continued writing poetry on a regular basis about life's many experiences, topics, and questions. It has become and remains to be a strong coping mechanism for me when dealing with "life." I have continued to develop and refine my writing abilities and have strengthened my art by adding, practicing, and improving on many tools in my toolbox, so to speak. Sharing these Christian poems has become my priority given today's troubling times with so many broken and lost people. Jesus is the answer to all of your questions!

Introduction

Welcome to the second volume of my Christian poetry collection. It is entitled *Let Me Save You: Poetic Bible Truths About Jesus Christ.* This collection focuses on Jesus Christ, His different roles and His special attributes, along with His important requirement for us as believers to be born again spiritually.

The first section in this book begins with Jesus. I try as best as I can to explain as many different aspects as possible of Jesus that have been revealed to me and what these most likely signify. Jesus is way too complex for us humans to fully understand Him. He is truly a mystery in and of Himself, given He is God Himself and part of the Trinity—one God existing as three parts (God the Father, God the Son, and God the Holy Spirit). But Jesus is special. He is 100 percent God but also 100 percent man. This is unheard of. Why would God surrender His holiness, His throne, His heaven for us? That's simple—God is love. God created us and He loves His creation, which is each one of us. But Adam fell, and thus all of mankind fell. God knew this would be. His plan was Jesus from the beginning. "Then God said, 'Let us make mankind in our image, in our likeness'" (Gen 1:26 NLT). Moreover, "In the beginning was the Word, and the Word was with God, and the Word was God" (John 1:1 NIV). "For by Him all things were created that are in heaven and that are on earth, visible and invisible, whether thrones or dominions or principalities or powers. All things were created through Him and for Him. And He is before all things, and in Him all things consist" (Col 1:16–17 NKJV).

I try to describe who Jesus is as detailed in the Holy Bible, some of His amazing characteristics, exactly what He did for us in the divine exchange, and some of the things He went through during His human lifetime, such as what he endured for us to set us all free from our sins to find salvation. Jesus is many things, but LORD and Savior are two of these that are the most important. "'The word is near you; it is in your mouth and in your heart,' that is, the message concerning faith that we proclaim: If you declare with your mouth, 'Jesus is Lord,' and believe in your heart that God raised him from the dead, you will be saved" (Rom 10:8–9 NIV). When in Christ, we have significant power and authority in this world. "Very truly I tell you, whoever believes in me will do the works I have been doing, and they will do even greater things than these, because I am going to the Father. And I will do whatever you ask in my name, so that the Father may be glorified in the Son. You may ask me for anything in my name, and I will do it" (John 14:12–14 NIV).

The second and final section of this book describes the need to be born again spiritually. This is also a very important requirement that God asks of His believers. "Repent and be baptized, every one of you, in the name of Jesus Christ for the forgiveness of your sins" (Acts 2:38 NIV). Furthermore, this is the Great Commission for His church, the sharing of the gospel to all people. "He said to them, 'Go into all the world and preach the gospel to all creation. Whoever believes and is baptized will be saved, but whoever does not believe will be condemned'" (Mark 16:15–16 NIV). Essentially, baptism is simply an outward sign of an inward (or internal) heart transformation. Your priorities are no longer your own but rather those of God's.

Thank you and may God bless you. Please enjoy!

JESUS

He Himself

(Adapted from the melody of "King's Cross" by Pet Shop Boys)

A man like no other sent on our behalf	John 5:30
Lowly He humbled Himself to surpass	Phil 2:5–8
He made Himself of no certain reputation	Phil 2:7
And predestined us to adoption	Eph 1:3–6
He even became obedient to death	Phil 2:7
Releasing His spirit with His final breath	Matt 27:50–51

He stripped Himself of glory	
He gave Himself a ransom	Phil 2:7; Mark 10:45
He Himself knew exactly what to do	John 6:6
He purchased us with His blood	
His sacrifice atoning	Gal 3:13–15
We're forever without blame and now surrounded with His love	
	Rom 5:1

The revelation only comes when you're lost	2 Cor 1:9
With nothing left but yourself exhaust	
Dead to your ego and then open your eyes	Rom 8:12–14
Once you believe, He'll never leave your side	John 10:28
Whether you're good or whether you're bad	
We're all guilty and we must decide	Rom 1:18–32

He stripped Himself of glory
He gave Himself a ransom
He Himself knew exactly what to do
He purchased us with His blood
His sacrifice atoning
We're forever without blame and now surrounded with His love

If you keep looking, then you will find	Matt 7:7
He'll freely give you His own supply	Matt 10:5–8
Surrender to His will and He'll increase	Matt 16:24–26
He Himself will become your peace	John 14:27
He'll reside within, gift you carte blanche	1 Cor 3:16
Regardless of the day or the circumstance	

He stripped Himself of glory
He gave Himself a ransom
He Himself knew exactly what to do
He purchased us with His blood
His sacrifice atoning
We're forever without blame and now surrounded with His love

And now we're surrounded with His love
We're surrounded with His love

Forgiven and Loved

We only care about ourselves
We post everything we do
Addicted to our smart phones, twenty-four hours through
    and through
How many "likes" do I have today? Posing for selfies; one, then two
I look so good scanning my profile
It's all about me, and not about you   2 Tim 3:2

Why do we act in this manner?
We all walk around so clueless
We don't even notice each other
A result of Satan's influence   2 Tim 3:2
Oblivious to the real world
We're distracted by all the machines
Numb to our surroundings
And disregarding our spiritual beings   Rom 7:18

He lays down His life   1 John 3:16
He receives all your sins   Heb 10:14
His death is so brutal   Matt 27:45-56
Contained within His skin   Heb 10:1-18
He was raised in three days   Luke 24:7
Prophecy fulfilled   1 Pet 1:19-20
You're completely forgiven   Heb 1:3
According to His will   Rom 12:2

It's time to change our minds
It's time for us to wake up   Luke 13:3
Somehow, we've lost our way
Our time on Earth's almost up   Matt 24:42-44
His return is forthcoming
This world has changed so much   Rev 3:11
We've turned our backs on Him
He'll be the judge of us   John 5:26-29

Being present in each moment
Putting others' needs first   Mark 12:31
Serving fellow human beings, unselfishness rehearsed
It's not how much we love Him
Rather, in us how much He loves   1 John 4:10
We can then love one another
When we truly know how much we're loved

He lays down His life
He receives all your sins
His death is so brutal
Contained within His skin
He was raised in three days
Prophecy fulfilled
You're completely forgiven
According to His will

It Is Written

(Adapted from the melody of "1-800-273-8255" by Logic, feat. Alessia Cara & Khalid)

After the river, My purpose defined	Matt 3:16
I now know what I've been assigned	1 Pet 2:24
I have to arise divine; heaven awaits	John 1:1–5

I don't wanna be deprived	
I just need to obey and pray	Luke 6:12
I just wanna comply	
I don't wanna be deprived	John 5:19
I just wanna comply	
Satan's wishes denied	Matt 4:1–11; Luke 4

My Father spoke highly of Me as He wrote it	Matt 3:17
I've been fasting for some time	
With temptation as I approach it	Matt 4:1–11
Preparing to defend	
I don't wanna to blow it, don't wanna blow it	Rom 3:24
Deep down inside I know I can't control it	Luke 22:42
Satan's asking Me for something as my stomach groans	
To make bread from a stone	
Just in an attempt to dethrone	Matt 4:3
Man does not live on bread alone, I recite	Matt 4:1–4
But rather every word that proceeds from God despite	

After the river, My purpose defined
I now know what I've been assigned
I have to arise divine; heaven awaits

After the river, My purpose defined
I now know what I've been assigned
I have to arise divine

I want all of you to arrive
I want all of you to arrive   1 Tim 2:4–6
You don't have to sigh today, You don't have to sigh
I want all of you to arrive, I want all of you to arrive
You don't have to sigh, now here's how you reply

Brought up to the Holy City   Matt 21:1–11
Set upon the pinnacle of the temple   Matt 21:12–17
And prove to me that you're the heir   Ps 2:7–8
Can you declare?   John 8:56–59
This would be instrumental
Throw yourself down, angels surround   Matt 4:1–11
Satan said these things if you are the Son of God   Matt 4:6
But I took a moment to respond
And I simply said instead
You shall not tempt the Lord your God   Matt 4:7

All the kingdoms of the world are yours if you worship me
                                                      Matt 4:8–9
You have the ability to rewrite
Get away from me Satan is what I recited   Matt 4:10
You shall worship the Lord your God   Matt 4:10
Him shall you serve   Matt 4:10
Only Him shall you serve
My faith in God I still vow   Matt 4:11
Thankfully, my faith in God I still vow

After the river, My purpose defined
I now know what I've been assigned
I have to arise divine; heaven awaits

After the river, My purpose defined
I now know what I've been assigned
I have to arise divine

My righteousness can be derived	
My righteousness can be derived	2 Cor 5:21
You just need to obey and pray	
You don't have to sigh	Rom 10:9
My righteousness can be derived	
My righteousness can be derived	
You don't have to sigh	
You don't have to sigh	

If you deny Christ, then you will certainly forego	1 John 2:22
And your soul will be lost you know	Rev 20:15
Reside in hell, paradise shut out	
Everlasting life frankly let go	

And you will surely die	Heb 9:27
Only for yourself account for	Rom 14:12
You will be denied	
Your choice determines what's in store	Rom 3:20
Oh, do you wanna?	
Do you wanna?	
Only you can answer for (yourself)	

Through Your Weakness

(Adapted from the melody of "Speechless" by Robin Schultz, feat. Erika Sirola)

I remember when you were discarded
Feeling desperate after so brokenhearted
And thinking this'll never happen to you again

I'm only seeking heirs	Rom 8:17
I know exactly how many hairs	Luke 12:7
Are present on your head	

If you love me, keep my commandments	John 14:15
Then you're aligned	
Obey my wishes, no more fighting	John 14:15–24
Intertwined	

Indeed, I love you	Matt 6:26
But you showed me your weakness when	Joel 2:32
That day you cried for me and said you loved me	John 21:15–19
Now you're aligned	

I remember how you stood guarded	
Several attempts to reach you were disregarded	
The constant barrage convinced you to surrender	Jas 4:7
Let go of keeping your own	1 Cor 6:19–20
Let's see all that I have in store	Jer 29:11
For you in due time	

If you love me, keep my commandments	
Then you're aligned	
Let me preside within, overriding	2 Cor 13:5
I will provide	Phil 4:19

LET ME SAVE YOU

Indeed, I love you
But you showed me your weakness when
That day you cried for me and said you loved me
Now, you're aligned

You showed your meekness   Col 3:12
Your uniqueness   Ps 139:13–14
No space between us   Jas 4:8

You couldn't dream this
The completeness   Col 2:10
You showed me your weakness   1 Cor 1:27
And all your secrets

If you love me, keep my commandments
Then you're aligned
A new life beginning   2 Cor 5:17
It's genius

Tow Truck

(Adapted from the melody of "Bad Habits" by Ed Sheeran)

Whenever your car breaks down, and when you're desperate for a tow
No rescue can be found, let alone a state patrol
The stress builds up beyond and I need to be consoled
I need to be saved, but is this futile?   Rom 6:23

The darkness covers like a fog, unbeknown
My imagination alters reality, soon overblown
Seeking any possible solution that might postpone
All of my helpless pursuits, deduce, excuses

The darkness blinds my eyes blocking all escapes
Questioning where I went wrong and all my mistakes
Retracing my steps from the start trying to erase
Not sure what else might ensue, accuse, undo
The darkness turns me towards You   Isa 9:2

The darkness turns me towards You
The darkness turns me towards You

The tow truck finally arrives and pulls forward to escort
In his cabin, knocks over a cup looking for the paperwork
I see the cross you display hoisted on the back of your truck
I'm reassured I'll no longer remain here stuck   1 Cor 1:18

The darkness scares me so despite the stoplight's glow
You're everything I wanted, everything I'd hoped
My spirit breathes a sigh of relief while you
        make your approach   Matt 11:28–30
Despite all of your tattoos, please excuse my views

Let Me Save You

The darkness surrounds me not knowing what really awaits
You write down all the info from my license plate
You make a copy of my credit card just in case
Then into the truck with you, us two, review

The darkness turns me towards You
The darkness turns me towards You

Just feeling secure is profound   Ps 91:1–4
I'm so happy that You I've found   Heb 12:1–2

The darkness dissipates suddenly on its own
The sun rises and then there's no more shadows
Coincidentally, I now feel much more in control
And then something lets me loose, produce, break through

The darkness served its purpose to show me
    Your grace   2 Cor 12:9
Out of danger and then a warm,
    gentle embrace   Jer 31:3; 1 John 3:1
No matter whatever I face
You'll always provide the escape   1 Cor 10:13
It's crystal clear in review, it's true, it's You   Phil 3:10–14
The darkness turns me towards You

No More Doubts

(Adapted from the melody of "Kids" by MGMT)

While in the river, suddenly emerging out	Matt 3:16
Distant behind a cloud	
God Himself spoke out loud	Matt 3:17
We're amazed with all of Jesus' actions	
He taught us things that were in contrast	Matt 5:1–48
To those in power with great impact	
Grace not withheld	Ps 84:11
For those willing to receive—no doubt	Mark 11:24
Sons and daughters appointed	2 Cor 6:18
Never disappointed	Ps 73:26
Falsehoods dispelled	Eph 4:25
Benefits transferred to our accounts	1 Cor 1:30
A sense of new belonging	Eph 2:13–15
To end prolonging	Matt 24:22
The norms are reformed	
But God's plan remains to deliver	Ps 34:17
A baby was born to die for our redemption	1 Tim 1:15
His intentions are to make clearer	
Soon a Savior draws nearer	Ps 73:28
With His death and indeed a very steep price	
You were willfully bought	1 Cor 6:19–20
Even with the mundane	
You're always in His thoughts	1 Pet 5:7
Virtue declared with the weak	
The mighty confounded	1 Cor 1:27–31
Righteousness is awarded	
Forever recorded	2 Sam 22:25

Heaven prepared	John 14:3
Just listen, as the trumpets sounded	1 Cor 15:51–57
A new government exported	Rev 19:16
Soon reordered	
Honor instilled	Heb 2:5–9
Solely based on Jesus' grounds	John 5:19
The fruits of the Spirit afforded	Gal 5:22–23
Until exhausted	
Beloved propelled	1 Cor 15:58
Conformed to His likeness	
Glory surrounded	2 Cor 3:18; Rom 8:29
With obedience and faith rewarded	Heb 11:6
So supported	Isa 41:10
Greatly excelled	Phil 2:9
Mount Zion is God's new mountain	Ps 125:1
Angels commanded, the saved are escorted	Ps 91:11
Quickly transported	1 Cor 15:52
Sonship upheld	
And then there were no more doubts	2 Cor 6:18
Thank you, God, for these!	Phil 4:5–7

Every Single Detail of the Cross

*(Adapted from the melody of "Elastic Heart" by Sia,
feat. Shia LaBeouf & Maddie Ziegler)*

Easter time's here, we must discuss	
God's ultimate plan from above	John 3:16
He had to turn His back; Jesus shunned	Isa 53:5–6
To forgive us and never be undone	Heb 9:15–22

Every particular, unique detail
That occurred during that time has prevailed
Each had its own significance
And not just any coincidence

Jesus died for you and me	John 3:17
In doing so, He made us free	John 8:36

Betrayed with a kiss right from the start	Luke 22:48
To the way He choose to die, depart	Matt 27:45–54
Stripped of His linen clothes	
Won by Roman guards	Matt 27:28–30
The sour wine that drenched His lips	Mark 15:36–37

And the countless ways that He was mocked	Matt 27:29
To the final words that He remarked	Luke 23:46
He had a special journey to embark	Matt 12:40
And He emerged as light from the dark	John 1:5

All the trials that took place at night	Mark 14:53
To the words "I am" that He'd recite	Mark 14:62
Cursed is He who hangs on the tree	Gal 3:13
That was the only way to guarantee	Acts 4:12; John 10:9

He was born to die, yes to die as a man	1 Tim 1:15
Pierced for our transgressions	Isa 53:5
The blade into His heart that was thrust	John 19:31–36
For our iniquities, He was crushed	Isa 53:5
On our behalf did He ever plead	Rom 8:34
Lest we get down on one knee	Phil 2:10–11
After His death, intact His legs were spared	John 19:31–36
Three days gone; a place prepared	John 14:3
And He had the power to lay down His life	
That He may take it up again	John 10:18
Resurrected body now repaired	Luke 24:39
Everlasting life has been declared	John 17:4
From Pilate's words that were nailed above His head	
Jesus the Nazarene . . .	John 19:19
Yud Hey Vav Hey is what it read	John 19:21
Just like on Christmas morn	Luke 2
When night became day, but condemned	Luke 2
Day became night instead	Matt 27:45–52
A crown of thorns and a scarlet robe	Matt 27:28–29
The saving grace for the entire globe	John 12:44–50
To be without sin yet becoming so exposed	2 Cor 5:21
Our Passover lamb	1 Cor 5:7
Our punishment has now been disposed of	Rom 8:1
To us, His righteousness has now been bestowed	2 Cor 5:21
Every single detail of the cross	

My Beloved Son

(Adapted from the melody of "Black Hole Sun" by Soundgarden)

I hear their cries, juxtaposed	Ps 40:1
I empathize, they're so exposed	Heb 4:15
I offer grace to ease their heartache	Eph 4:7
To fix their errors, a warm embrace	Jer 31:3
Future's bleak, they fear revenge	Rom 12:19
So, I speak; their thirst is quenched	Isa 44:3–13
There's no blame, I redeem	Heb 9:12
Because I reign supreme—Amen	Exod 15:18
My beloved Son overcomes	John 16:33
Christ is coming again!	Matt 24:42–44
My beloved Son overcomes, overcomes, overcomes	
Muttering? He's the lamp	Rev 22:5
The Law's rescinded, there is no lack	Col 2:14; Ps 34:9
Please press on, be born again	John 3:5–7
A phenomenon takes shape	
You must choose to be His sheep	John 10:27–28
This is the truth: you sow what you reap	Gal 6:7–9
Don't pretend	
You're not prey	1 Pet 5:8
Live victoriously furthermore	Jas 4:7; 1 John 5:4
My beloved Son overcomes	
Christ is coming again!	
My beloved Son overcomes, overcomes	
He's the bread, don't you fear	John 6:35
So that you can now approach Me near	Eph 3:12

My beloved Son overcomes
Christ is coming again!
My beloved Son overcomes, overcomes

My beloved Son overcomes
Christ is coming again!
My beloved Son overcomes, overcomes

It Happened at Night

(Adapted from the melody of "I'm Good (Blue)" by David Guetta & Bebe Rexha)

It happened; He was born at night	Luke 2:8
Despite the darkness and likewise despite the quiet	
In an animal's manger He was hidden from sight	Luke 2:12
Angels were singing glory to the world's delight	Luke 2:13–14
The black night quickly changed to bright	Luke 2:9
What a blessing that Jesus became the world's light	John 8:12
He would grow up and His ministry would ignite	Luke 4:15
And provide a way for us and God to reunite	Rom 5:10–11

It's good, good, good
It happened; He was born at night

Because of Jesus, we have His birthright	John 1:12
This was God's plan, His foresight	John 3:16
He exists outside of time, He's infinite	Gen 1:14–19
Indeed, Jesus roamed near the Dead Sea	2 Kgs 14:25
He cursed the fig tree near Bethany	Mark 11:12–25
Thanks be to God that we're set free	1 Pet 5:7–14

It happened; He was born at night
Despite the darkness and likewise despite the quiet
In an animal's manger He was hidden from sight
Angels were singing glory to the world's delight

It's good, good, good
It happened, He was born at night

Right Where You Are

(Adapted from the melody of "Rockstar" by Post Malone, feat. 21 Savage)

Jesus will always find you	
and meet you right where you are	John 20:19–31
Jesus will always listen	
and respond to all of your prayers	1 John 5:14
Jesus will always guide you	
and shine bright as the North Star	Matt 2:9
Jesus will provide you skills	
and wisdom to build a repertoire	2 Pet 1:3–4
Jesus will always be with	
you like riding in a side car	Matt 28:20
Jesus will always do the work	
but give you credit as His co-star	John 3:27
Jesus will always be accessible	
through His Word in His memoir	John 20:29
Jesus in first place means	
your life won't get much darker	John 8:12; Isa 9:2
Whenever you find yourself in trouble or in a jam	
Don't let Satan trick or deceive you; it's a scam	John 8:44
A counterfeit sham	
Satan will try to tempt you with a real enticing exam	Jas 1:14
But Jesus provides the way out; He's the sacrificial lamb	
So, adopt His program	1 Cor 10:13

Jesus will always find you and meet you right where you are
Jesus will always listen and respond to all of your prayers
Jesus will always guide you and shine bright as the North Star
Jesus will provide you skills and wisdom to build a repertoire

And when He takes actions in your life
You will be left in awe   Eccl 5:7
You will be under grace and
    no longer fall under the law   Rom 6:14
Things will start to come easy
And you will find results—voila!   Matt 11:28–30
He'll love you like a son
And you'll love Him like a father   2 Cor 6:18

Put on your armor and prepare for combat   Eph 6:10–18
Look to Him for help or you might fall flat   Isa 41:10
And protect yourself from treacherous hazmat   Isa 54:17
Simplify your life; don't be a pack rat   1 Tim 6:6–10

Meet you right where you are
He's a present-day czar
Certainly, without a doubt
He will help you mature   Col 1:28–29
Great things He'll usher
And you will feel so secure   Ps 91:9–12
Meet you right where you are
He'll meet you right where you are

Jesus will always find you and meet you right where you are
Jesus will always listen and respond to all of your prayers
Jesus will always guide you and shine bright as the North Star
Jesus will provide you skills and wisdom to build a repertoire

Jesus will meet you right where you are

Soon in Paradise

(Adapted from the melody of "Gangsta's Paradise" by Coolio)

As soon as we're born, there'll be a last breath   Heb 9:27
Our lives may take different paths
But the end's always your best guess
He causes situations to help you examine what's wrong
To redirect your life versus why you're withdrawn   Rom 8:28

God sacrificed His Son's life just to preserve it   John 3:16
The price of sin is eternal death, but He reversed it   Rom 6:23
Each day, it's wise to use caution; or you'll be forgotten
Must believe in Jesus Christ to become God's begotten
                                        John 5:24; Prov 3:4

You need to realize that we're all broke   John 15:5
And that Jesus evokes assistance, His easy yoke   Matt 11:30
Satan will do everything possible to indict   Rev 12:10
Jesus will make things right
He received your penalties despite   Rom 8:3

I'm the ultimate sacrifice; you'll be with me soon in paradise
I'm the ultimate sacrifice; you'll be with me soon in paradise
I'm the ultimate sacrifice; you'll be with me soon in paradise
I'm the ultimate sacrifice; you'll be with me soon in paradise
                                        Luke 23:43

Two other men were crucified and waiting   Luke 23:32
For their painful death
They were intentionally displayed   Luke 23:33
Each represents two opposite extremes
Their conversations shared with Jesus in-between

The unrepentant thief blatantly maligned
"Come down from the cross" he sarcastically opined   Luke 23:39
He spoke with such ignorance and with such insulting rancor
Not knowing that Jesus would become the world's anchor

Ps 34:17

While the other thief rebuked the former one that day
Instead, he asked Jesus if it would be okay
If he could be taken up with Christ in His shadow
"Today, you'll be with Me"; this I know   Luke 23:40–43
If you want to be free, then seek His mercy   Ps 51
Proclaim Christ's innocence, then it's guaranteed

1 Pet 3:18; Rom 10:9–11

I'm the ultimate sacrifice; you'll be with me soon in paradise
I'm the ultimate sacrifice; you'll be with me soon in paradise
I'm the ultimate sacrifice; you'll be with me soon in paradise
I'm the ultimate sacrifice; you'll be with me soon in paradise

It's a riveting study, this one chance encounter
One of them damned; the other man towered
One refused judgment, forgiveness overlooked him
While the second man received grace that overtook him

Luke 23:41

Blessed is he who yearns
Who asks God to "Redeem me"   Isa 44:21–23
Whoever gives up their life for Jesus will receive it   Matt 10:39
Just like it's wrote, if you revolt, then it's on you
You'll be stranded alone without a lifeboat   Gal 6:3

I'm the ultimate sacrifice; you'll be with me soon in paradise
I'm the ultimate sacrifice; you'll be with me soon in paradise
I'm the ultimate sacrifice; you'll be with me soon in paradise
I'm the ultimate sacrifice; you'll be with me soon in paradise

If you want to be free, then seek His mercy
Proclaim Christ's innocence, then it's guaranteed

Forty Lashes

(Adapted from the melody of "Say It Right" by Nelly Furtado)

It's not good, it's not right	
In plain sight, He was mauled	Matt 27:26
Forty lashes, exposed bone	Deut 25:3
One stripe left for us all	Isa 53:5–6
His whole body was broken	Isa 53:5–6
All of this was God's plan	John 1:11–13
"Please forgive" is what was spoken	Luke 23:34
As nails pierced his hands	Luke 23:33
Why'd You choose this instead of punishing me?	
Why'd You allow Jesus to die on that tree?	Gal 3:13
Why'd You turn Your back on Jesus just for me?	Ps 22
Why'd You choose this instead of punishing me?	
He's the way and the light	
The truth—by the cross	John 14:6
And He paid the full price	
To purchase us—we exalt	1 Cor 6:20, 7:23
All His life, He atoned	
He chose to live deprived	1 John 2:2
So, through His ordeal	
He would bestow the gift of life (gift of life)	Rom 6:23
Why'd You choose this instead of punishing me?	
Why'd You allow Jesus to die on that tree?	
Why'd You turn Your back on Jesus just for me?	
Why'd You choose this instead of punishing me?	

Holes in His hands, a wound in His side;   John 20:26–27
His bloodied body was displayed
Then dark clouds and cries continued;
We're fortunate He obeyed   Luke 23:44–46
He embodied God's wrath
    to undo—by His grace   1 Pet 2:24; Gal 3:13; John 3:16
He was unclothed, forgiven fully;   Matt 27:28–35
He and I were transposed

Why'd You choose this instead of punishing me?
Why'd You choose this instead of punishing me?

Past Offerings

(Adapted from the melody of "100 Ways" by Jackson Wang)

A ransom of your sins past	Matt 20:28
An ox, a lamb, or turtledove perhaps to undo, undo	Lev 5:7
This judgment's done in contrast	
These are frequent and minor and can't surpass. Bring two?	
	Lev 5:7

You don't have to be ashamed	
You are made right and reclaimed	Rom 1:16

There's only one way to	
really cover, really cover, really cover	1 John 1:7
Only one way to really cover, really cover, really cover	

There's only one way to really cover.	
How big's your faith? Is it stronger?	Matt 17:20–21
Only one way to really cover	
This is what He has guaranteed	Rom 4:16

Jesus has replaced these all	Rom 5:18
These are void; He, we exalt—brand new, brand new	
	2 Cor 5:17

Every single past assault	Isa 53:6
All these upon Himself he brought, ooh	2 Cor 5:21
And yes, we've been ordained; free from guilt proclaimed	
	Eph 1:7

There's only one way to really cover, really cover, really cover
Only one way to really cover, really cover, really cover

There's only one way to really cover
How big's your faith? Is it stronger?
Only one way to really cover
This is what He has guaranteed
This is what He has guaranteed

There's only one way to really cover, really cover, really cover
Only one way to really cover, really cover, really cover

There's only one way to really cover
How big's your faith? Is it stronger?
Only one way to really cover
This is what He has guaranteed
This is what He has guaranteed

God Became Man

(Adapted from the melody of "Circle In the Sand"
by Belinda Carlisle)

Angels sound, He's been crowned	Heb 2:5–9
Heaven used to be His domain	Ps 115
At last, God turned His back	Matt 27:46
This is what He has ordained	Acts 2:23
To Him, everything we have is owed	Rom 11:36
Jesus is the perfect measure	Heb 10:12
Believe in Him, He resides within	John 11:25; Gal 2:20
Our souls He treasures	Deut 7:6;
God became man, this is so profound	John 1:14
A warm golden glow for believers surrounds	
	Heb 12:1; Rev 14:1
And Jesus' crucifixion supersedes	Matt 27:32–56
Eternity is guaranteed	John 3:16
God became man, God became man	
Deadly sins, now have been	Heb 9:26
He suffered great in despair	Matt 27:27–31
God forsake; He took our place	2 Cor 5:14
Righteousness, you can now declare	2 Cor 5:21
Triunity—God is one, but three	Gen 1:26; Matt 28:19–20
Flesh was His endeavor	John 1:14
He descended so that we can depend	Eph 4:9–10
Strong faith possessors	1 Cor 3:21
God became man, this is so profound	
Forget this earth, grow your heavenly account	Matt 6:19–21

And all you have to do is receive   Mark 11:24
His blessings will exceed   2 Cor 9:8
God became man, God became man

God hears all of our pleas
His love is so restoring   1 John 5:14; 1 Pet 5:10

To Him, everything we have is owed
Jesus is the perfect measure
Believe in Him, He resides within
Our souls He treasures

God became man, this is so profound
A warm golden glow for believers surrounds
And all you have to do is receive
His blessings will exceed

God became man, God became man
God became man, God became man

31

God's Son

(Adapted from the melody of "Numb" by Marshmello & Khalid)

Who do you want to become?
Receive what's been done?   Phil 1:4–6
Focus on the prize, keep your eyes on God's Son   Col 2:10
He's the bread of life for some; He is when time begun   John 6:35
Who do you want to become? A son, son, son?
                                                     John 1:12; Gal 3:26

Who do you want to become? Receive what's been done?
Focus on the prize, keep your eyes on God's Son
He's the bread of life for some; He is when time begun
Who do you want to become? A son, son, son?

Who do you want to become? Lazy?
Self-righteous and inflated?
Lost and desecrated?
Or worst yet heaven unrelated?

Too sensitive and jaded?
Morally bankrupt and degraded?
Spiritually dead and then fake it?
Destined for hell—forsaken?   Rev 20:15

Who do you want to become? Receive what's been done?
Focus on the prize, keep your eyes on God's Son
He's the bread of life for some; He is when time begun
Who do you want to become? A son, son, son?

Blessed are those who are blind yet see   John 20:29
Blessed are those who are deaf yet hear   Isa 29:18; Matt 11:5
He's the light of the world
And the resurrection of the dead   John 8:12
Place your trust in Him instead   Prov 3:5–6

Who do you want to become? Receive what's been done?
Focus on the prize, keep your eyes on God's Son
He's the bread of life for some; He is when time begun
Who do you want to become? A son, son, son?

Who do you want to become? Receive what's been done?
Focus on the prize, keep your eyes on God's Son
He's the bread of life for some; He is when time begun
Who do you want to become? A son, son, son?

Who Will You Ultimately Trust?

(Adapted from the melody of "Uprising" by Muse)

Witnessing the empty tomb	John 20:1–18
He knew us before he formed us in the womb	Jer 1:5
All the miracles	Mark 5:25–34; John 9:1–11; Matt 15:32–38
And wonders that astound	
To our final judgment from God cast down	
	Heb 9:27; 2 Cor 5:10

He's an advocate, a go-between	1 John 2:1
His grace is sufficient, His death exceeds	Rom 5:17
All your needs will be met, He'll align	Ps 37:4; 2 Pet 1
He's morally strong; He'll be your guide	Col 3:15–25

When things are in flux	
Who can redeem the unjust?	Gal 3:13
Dust will return to dust	
Who will you ultimately trust?	Eccl 3:20

He cares about saving your soul	1 Tim 2:4–6
Regardless of what happens, He's in control	Ps 103:19
If you place your faith and trust in Him whereby	Prov 3:5–6
And live your life for others to glorify	
	1 Pet 4:10–11; Rom 12:10

He will ensure you possess no lack	Ps 34:9–10
His bloodshed has purchased you back	1 Cor 6:20
You'll need a child's heart to comprehend	Matt 18
He's all you need; you're no longer condemned	Rom 8:1–17

When things are in flux
Who can redeem the unjust?
Dust will return to dust
Who will you ultimately trust?

Our Attorney

(Adapted from the melody of "Easy On Me" by Adele)

You know there's only one who can forgive	Heb 9:22
Who has the ability to save us and deliver	1 Pet 1:19, 2:22

There's only one scapegoat for sons and daughters	Rom 8:3
Who was also present at the beginning	John 1:1
Who speaks and things appear and fully compliant	Gen 1:3
And who lives within	Rom 8:10

Jesus is our attorney	1 John 2:1
Turns to me and smiles	Luke 10:21; Luke 15:11–32
And He can see right through	Ps 53:2; Ps 44:21

Kneel; sin no longer controls me	Rom 6:14
Jesus was crushed and bruised	Isa 53:5
And not just for the Jews	2 Cor 5:14–15
Jesus is our attorney	

There's been an amazing, divine exchange	Gal 1:11–16, 2:20
On our behalf, it has already been carefully arranged	
	John 3:16–17

You've already died when Jesus Christ died	Rom 6:6
Surrender to Him and live out His plan for your life	Jer 29:11
Your faith is your trust	Heb 11:1

Jesus is our attorney
Turns to me and smiles
And He can see right through

Kneel; sin no longer controls me
Jesus was crushed and bruised
And not just for the Jews
Jesus is our attorney
The cross is our receipt   1 Cor 1:18

He wants to provide for us   Phil 4:19
And so easy is His yoke   Matt 11:28–30
But you can deny   Mark 8:38; Matt 10:33
Without Him, you're spiritually broke   1 John 2:22; 1 John 1:9

Jesus is our attorney
Turns to me and smiles
And He can see right through

Kneel; sin no longer controls me
Jesus was crushed and bruised
And not just for the Jews
Jesus is our attorney

He Felt Our Anguish

(Adapted from the melody of "East Side" by Benny Blanco, Halsey & Khalid)

Although divine, He came from above	Ps 115
Delivered for our sake, we're His beloved	2 Tim 1:9
He was always full of compassion	Matt 9:36
Even though He was part God, part human made of	Phil 2:6–8

He could heal anyone
With His touch   Matt 8:14–16; Mark 1:29–34; Luke 4:38–41
He was special, God's one and only Son   John 3:16
With His obedience, sacrifice, and mercy   John 6:38
He opened the flood gates   Acts 2:1–47

It's significant that He cried   Matt 27:46
He carries our burdens, don't forge   1 Pet 5:7; Matt 11:28–30
We're the church and we're His bride   Eph 5:22–33
Our lives are shaped fondly from the outset

You could find Jesus as He prayed at first light   Mark 1:35
The wages of sin surely did haunt   Rom 6:23
He wouldn't stop until it was complete   John 19:30
Pierced both His hands, His feet
We're free—yeah   Isa 53:5

He became our sin debt, took our place
God did permit   1 John 2:2
Jesus values our friendship   Prov 17:17; Jas 4:7–10
Preparing for the cross
He would indeed submit   Phil 2:8; Matt 26:39
His sweat dripped with blood for our benefit   Luke 22:44

Lazarus was dead for four days   John 11:17
Mary and Martha distraught; "Move the stone away"   John 11:39
Jesus groaned in the spirit and was troubled   John 11:33, 38

Jesus cried, cried with thee   John 11:35

Never seen, His death was a calamity
With pain and suffering, he'd intervene
And now, triumphantly
We're allowed in God's company   2 Cor 5:21
What a privilege, now and for eternity   John 5:24

Sitting at God's right hand, Jesus paved the way   Col 3:1
His footstool comprised His enemies   Ps 110:1
Today, there is so much power in the tongue   Prov 18:21
You can build and heal others just because it's done   Eph 4:29
It's significant that He cried
He carries our burdens, don't forget
We're the church and we're His bride
Our lives are shaped fondly from the outset

You could find Jesus as He prayed at first light
The wages of sin surely did haunt
He wouldn't stop until it was complete
Pierced both His hands, His feet; we're free
He's so forgiving
                Luke 5:20; Luke 7:47–48; Matt 9:1–8; Mark 2:1–12

He became our sin debt, took our place; God did permit
Jesus values our friendship
Preparing for the cross, He would indeed submit
His sweat dripped with blood for our benefit

Lazarus was dead for four days
Mary and Martha distraught; "Move the stone away"
Jesus groaned in the spirit and was troubled
Jesus cried, cried with thee

Jesus cried, wow!
It's significant that He cried
He carries our burdens, don't forget

Aleph and Tav

(Adapted from the melody of "Fireflies" by Owl City)

Jesus's signature has been disguised
Let me share what this signifies
It can be found if you are willing to seek

Just ask Him in your prayers   John 14:13–17
He can certainly be found anywhere   Isa 41:10
It's hidden in the Bible where aleph and tav are paired

The Holy Spirit will indwell, you'll conceive
This revelation will be shared, you'll receive
The "first and the last"
Or the "alpha and omega" in Greek   Rev 22:13
He exists outside of time, a mystery   John 1:3; Heb 1:2

Never utter His name because
The Jews deemed it too Holy; and it was
Not anyone of them would
Take the chance   Exod 20:7; Rom 8:15–16

The first verse in the Bible read   John 1:1
Right in the middle, He's embedded
There together in the beginning as one triune Godhead
     Matt 28:19

Aleph and tav are purposefully weaved
Bookmarks to the entire Bible pre-conceived
They're also bookmarks
in the Book of Revelation indeed   Rev 22:13
Because healing's in Jesus' bloodstream   Isa 53:4–5
It's the Bible's theme

Before creation, there existed pitch black   Gen 1:2
(Patiently waiting for You to appear)
Light became, but thereafter man's setback   Gen 1:3
(Patiently waiting for You to appear)
Many people have since been suffering steep
(Patiently waiting for You to appear)
Jesus is coming soon to shepherd His sheep   John 10:27–28

In His name, we baptize   Matt 28:18–20
And our lives transform likewise   Rom 12:2
"The One who was, and is, and is to come" will serve well
                          Rev 1:4–7

When aleph and tav are there
They're untranslated but declare
"Thy kingdom come" as noted in the Lord's Prayer   Matt 6:10

It says that they will look on Me,
Whom they have pierced, and grieve bitterly   Isa 53:5
And hidden deep within the twenty-two letter Hebrew alphabet
Besides numbers, the letters are stamped as pictures in fact

Aleph is an ox that intervenes
He bears the yoke and it's light and easy   Matt 11:28–30
Tav is a cross where the Lamb was slain
for the world in order to redeem   1 Cor 28–31
Wherein salvation can be achieved for eternity   John 3:16

Aleph and tav are purposefully weaved
Bookmarks to the entire Bible pre-conceived
They're also bookmarks in the Book of Revelation indeed
Because healing's in Jesus' bloodstream

These Silver Dollars

(Adapted from the melody of "Little Wonders" by Rob Thomas)

Long ago
Of all things, Jesus was the upholder
Foreshadowed   Isa 53
Because God is the ultimate controller   Eph 1:11
Gone with sin   Rom 6:5–8
His death and resurrection have renewed   2 Cor 4:16
It begins
For the Righteousness of God has been revealed   2 Cor 5:21

Jesus was sold for these silver dollars   Matt 26:14–16
Thirty pieces of coinage
And because of this, prosperity awaits   3 John 1:2

Judas betrayed for these silver dollars
These silver dollars, please let me explain

You must decide
Your life, the love of money can undo   1 Tim 6:10
You must align
Instead, an eternal currency choose   Matt 6:20
And what about in-kind?
You must be careful in all that you pursue   1 John 2:15–17
He'll supply all your needs in His riches
And glory and then you'll ascend   Phil 4:19

The rich man in Hades by his own power   Luke 16:19–31
Could only grumble by himself without his estate
No more delaying for these silver dollars
These silver dollars, please abstain

Please do not covet   Exod 20:17
Tight hands mean a small flow
God will surely offset
Allow money to flow through thou

These silver dollars, thirty pieces of coinage
And because of this, prosperity awaits
And because of this, prosperity awaits

Don't go astray for these silver dollars
These silver dollars, He'll sustain

You and Jesus have exchanged   2 Cor 5:21
Thirty pieces of coinage
And because of this, prosperity awaits

Blessings underway, these silver dollars   Num 6:24–26
Thirty pieces of coinage
He'll arrange   Rom 8:28

Breakthrough

(Adapted from the melody of "Wild Blue" by John Mayer)

Witnessing the cross's horror	Matt 27:32–56
Seeing God's judgment poured	
	Rom 3:24–25; Gal 3:13
Trying to understand all of this	
And what exactly did He commit?	2 Cor 5:21

Oh, breakthrough, Jesus provided an avenue	
Breakthrough because He obeyed	John 6:38
He loved us to give us a breakthrough	
He died so that we can live in lieu	John 3:17

All the things that He denied	Matt 19:23
The opposite to us implied	
Where there's two, there's now three	Acts 2:1–4
That's God's grace and God's mercy	John 1:17; Eph 2:4

Oh, breakthrough, Jesus provided an avenue
Breakthrough because He obeyed
He loved us to give us a breakthrough
He died so that we can live in lieu

Breakthrough, Jesus provided an avenue
Breakthrough because He obeyed
He loved us to give us a breakthrough
He died so that we can live in lieu

He joined on the road	
Broke and blessed bread, then gave, and then bestowed	
	John 6:35

Just Ask In Jesus' Name

(Adapted from the melody of "Sweetest Pie" by Megan Thee Stallion & Dua Lipa)

Ooh, when you're feeling down and blue; push through

Ooh, when you've been jack-knifed
When you encounter some strife
When someone tries to incite; just ask in Jesus' name

John 14:13–14

Ooh, when you're getting harassed
When you're physically bashed
Realize that you're in last; just ask in Jesus' name   Matt 5:3–16

If you need a loan—resist
You're accident prone—dismiss
Suddenly you're dethroned; just ask in Jesus' name

Ooh, when you're frustrated with life
When you struggle with your wife
Can't fall asleep at night; just ask in Jesus' name

When things are the bleakest
When you feel the weakest   1 Cor 1:29
When the next mountain
You encounter is the steepest   Matt 17:20
Without a shovel in a hole that's the deepest
Cross paths with another who treats you the meanest

When things are postponed, when you feel all alone
When you're really exhausted, when stress gets overblown
One thing after another, you moan and groan
There's no end in sight, the future's unknown

Your body pays a price, pack it in ice
No luck, just throw the dice
Nothing, nothing really seems to suffice
Looking for anything that excites

Money's real tight, nothing's ever enough
Nothing comes easy, overwhelming stuff
It's Murphy's Law, and you're handcuffed

Ooh, when you've been jack-knifed
When you encounter some strife
When someone tries to incite; just ask in Jesus' name

Ooh, when you're getting harassed
When you're physically bashed
Realize that you're in last; just ask in Jesus' name

If you need a loan—resist
You're accident prone—dismiss
Suddenly you're dethroned; just ask in Jesus' name
Ooh, when you're frustrated with life
When you struggle with your wife
Can't fall asleep at night; just ask in Jesus' name

Just because you're stuck, don't just presume
Tomorrow, another day will certainly bloom   Matt 6:34
With prayer and supplication, you're immune   Phil 4:6
Soon, your life will resume

Announce: Satan renounce   Jas 4:7
God has filled your account   1 Tim 6:17
In His presence, you stand on hallowed ground   Exod 3:5
He'll direct your path to rebound   Prov 16:9
You'll finally have plenty; the drought is gone   Phil 4:11–13

LET ME SAVE YOU

Regardless of what is, God permits	Heb 6:3
You are worthy as long as you submit	Jas 4:7
Share your heart, to the LORD commit	Prov 16:3,9
He took your place; God acquits	1 Pet 3:18

When you're feeling down and blue; push through

Ooh, when you've been jack-knifed
When you encounter some strife
When someone tries to incite; just ask in Jesus' name

Ooh, when you're getting harassed
When you're physically bashed
Realize that you're in last; just ask in Jesus' name
If you need a loan—resist
You're accident prone—dismiss
Suddenly you're dethroned; just ask in Jesus' name

Ooh, when you're frustrated with life
When you struggle with your wife
Can't fall asleep at night, just ask in Jesus' name

Ooh, when you're frustrated with life
When you struggle with your wife
Can't fall asleep at night; just ask in Jesus' name

Pray In Jesus' Name

(Adapted from the melody of "Ride Wit Me" by Nelly)

Want impact? Want impact? Want impact? Want impact?

If you wanna know the secret to enrich greatly	Ps 65:9
I could talk for hours, though I'll keep it pithy	
Why don't you pray in Jesus' name?	John 14:13–14
It's already been done. You see?	John 19:30

If you wanna flow with the Spirit and succeed	John 7:38–39
And in every aspect of your life exceed	Phil 4:19
Why don't you pray in Jesus' name?	
It's already been done. You see?	

In your bed with the moonlight at midnight
Searching for some answers and any insight
Trying to find a way forward because you feel so alone
Others offered to help, but you refused
"Should I reconsider?," you conclude
You come to the realization that there's nowhere left to turn
You're screwed
Jump out of bed, find a shirt in the dresser drawer
Bored and lost, you want to leave home and look for
Sneak out the back door
Grab some cash to pay for
Whatever you can find at the local convenience store
You still find yourself in such despair
You need to explore elsewhere

You remember as a kid the Lord's Prayer	Matt 6:9–13

And now there's an end to your nightmare

If you wanna know the secret to enrich greatly
I could talk for hours, though I'll keep it pithy
Why don't you pray in Jesus' name?
It's already been done. You see?

If you wanna flow with the Spirit and succeed
And in every aspect of your life exceed
Why don't you pray in Jesus' name?
It's already been done. You see?

You wish you could retract all the things in your past
Have a do over and begin again with a fresh start in fact
Avoid becoming entrapped and always under attack   Eph 6:12
Instead of possessing an everlasting contract   Eccl 3:9–14
God doesn't want you in combat
Nor to be become prey   1 Pet 5:8–9
There's been an exchange, it's already arranged   John 1:12

This is explained now
You're no longer empty or drained, but sustained now   Phil 4:19
He'll do it to glorify His Son, you're ordained now   Jer 1:5
And there's no blame now   Col 1:21–22
Nothing left to feel outraged about
You're center stage now
No more complaints now
Do you understand how?
If you believe, then you'll receive   Matt 21:22
This is grace and God's mercy, you're so worthy   Matt 6:26
He's our attorney throughout this journey
     Heb 7:25; Rom 8:34
Returning to God, reunite   Eccl 12:7
Your future becomes bright
All this according to His will and purpose
It'll be alright   Rom 8:28

If you wanna know the secret to enrich greatly
I could talk for hours, though I'll keep it pithy
Why don't you pray in Jesus' name?
It's already been done. You see?

If you wanna flow with the Spirit and succeed
And in every aspect of your life exceed
Why don't you pray in Jesus' name?
It's already been done. You see?

You're a wreck, wreck

The Holy Spirit surrounds and glows	Heb 12:1–2; Ps 34:7
It's not about your behavior	Isa 64:6
A crown of pure gold	
Splendor and majesty bestowed	2 Tim 4:8; 1 Pet 5:4; Rev 2:10
Jesus becomes your savior	1 John 4:14
Then His supply and countless blessings	
Begin to overflow	Ps 23:5
From now on you'll find favor	Luke 2:52

Success enters your life and no more status quo	
Jesus delivers so much greater	John 6:51
Guess what? You're a Christian hereby	
Please now be assured	1 John 5:13
Your soul and spirit will mature	2 Cor 3:18
Your flesh has been cured	Gal 5:24
Be secure, saved for sure	John 3:16
Let Him be your teacher	Luke 24:27
Grateful that you're a believer	1 Tim 2:4–6
Eventually become a preacher	Matt 28:19–20
As one of His beloved creatures	Gen 1:27
You don't have to try to comprehend	Isa 55:8

Guard your heart and mind
As the peace of God transcends   John 14:27
So, if you're really gonna get caught, get caught in the hit or miss
And if you really wanna stop, yes stop to reminisce
And if you don't wanna get lost, get lost in the abyss
Surely, you're gonna want the crisis, the crisis to cease

Talk the talk, He is risen   2 Cor 4
Walk the walk, a new mission   2 Cor 5:17
He just needs your permission   Gal 2:20
In order to supply His provision   2 Cor 9:8
So that your life will flourish   Ps 115:14
Bear much fruit and nourish   Matt 7:15–20
To be a blessing for others on the premise   Prov 11:25; 1 Pet 3:9
And finally get what you wished   Ps 37:4

If you wanna know the secret to enrich greatly
I could talk for hours, though I'll keep it pithy
Why don't you pray in Jesus' name?
It's already been done. You see?

If you wanna flow with the Spirit and succeed
And in every aspect of your life exceed
Why don't you pray in Jesus' name?
It's already been done. You see?

If you wanna flow with the Spirit and succeed
And in every aspect of your life exceed
Why don't you pray in Jesus' name?
It's already been done. You see?

For Our Benefit

(Adapted from the melody of "Take My Name" by Parmalee)

So, Jesus died; this was God's design	1 Cor 1:18–19
He took our place, for this defines	2 Cor 5:14
We can now approach God for sure	Jas 4:8
His righteousness, Jesus ensured	2 Cor 5:21

He laid down his life and He rose from the dead	Matt 28:5–6
He showed everyone His wounds	John 20:27
He ascended to heaven	
And is seated at God's right-hand	Luke 24:51; 1 Pet 3:22
His actions have atoned	Gal 1:4

God is holy and the price of sin's death	Rom 6:23
No matter what, we will all fall short	Rom 3:23
But today, Jesus acts as our advocate	Rom 8:34
To us, His rights have been transferred	1 Cor 1:30

So, Jesus died; this was God's design
He took our place, for this defines
We can now approach God for sure
His righteousness, Jesus ensured

With His own blood, Jesus purchased our lives	1 Cor 6:20
He voluntarily took our place	Phil 2:8
He retrieved hell's keys	
And we belong to Him	Rev 1:17–18; Eph 2:13–15
The Holy Spirit now indwells	1 Cor 3:16

We are God's righteousness through Christ	2 Cor 5:21
We can be near Him, affectionate	Jas 4:8
Jesus refutes so many accusations	Rom 8:34
He does this for our benefit	1 Cor 1:30

So, Jesus died; this was God's design
He took our place, for this defines
We can now approach God for sure
His righteousness, Jesus ensured

I'm not that smart, but take my advice
You might want to accept His invite   Rev 3:20
You can risk damnation if you prefer   John 8:24
But with Him, eternal life's conferred   John 3:16

It's not your fault   Rom 8:28
Think twice when you're under attack   1 Pet 5:8
You've been called   Rom 1:6
Let Jesus do the work in contrast   Matt 11:28–30

Jesus died; this was God's design
He took our place, for this defines
We can now approach God for sure
His righteousness, Jesus ensured

I'm not that smart, but take my advice
You might want to accept His invite
You can risk damnation if you prefer
But with Him, eternal life's conferred

Jesus ensured   Heb 7:22
You can risk damnation if you prefer
But with Him, eternal life's conferred

Noel

(Adapted from the melody of "Greedy" by Tate McRae)

God's ways are so mysterious	Isa 55:8–11
Jesus was born and wrapped in a cloth	Luke 2:12; Matt 1:21
Darkness suddenly became light	Luke 2:9
Then He was placed in a feeding trough	Luke 2:7
What exactly was happening?	
Descended from the line of David's house	Matt 1:1; Luke 2:4
Peace to those on whom His favor rests	Luke 2:14
It was the LORD Himself	Luke 2:11
Are we just dreaming?	
God in flesh to dwell	John 1:14
The shepherds praising	Luke 2:8–9; Luke 2:20
Good news, joyous Noel	John 1:14
Others will be seeking	Matt 2
His grace not withheld	Ps 84:11
I'm overwhelmed	
Years later—after He died, they found	
No body present in Joseph's tomb	Matt 27:57; Luke 23:50
His linens were arranged on the ground	Luke 24:12
Two angels in white, they proclaimed	
Woman, why are you crying?	Matt 28:5
Soon, Jesus's hands and side displayed	John 20:20
He breathed the Holy Spirit and then broke bread	John 20:22

It was the LORD Himself
Are we just dreaming?
God in flesh to dwell
The shepherds praising
Good news, joyous Noel
Others will be seeking
His grace not withheld
I'm overwhelmed

Jesus is so glorious	Heb 1:3
He was born to die in fact	1 Tim 1:15
We're all called to be saintly	1 Cor 1:1–2
We'll have victory over death	1 Cor 15:54–55; Rom 8:38–39
It's that simple quite plainly	
All you have to do is accept	Rom 10:9
Then you He'll resurrect someday	
	John 11:25–26; 1 Cor 15:20–22

It was the LORD Himself
Are we just dreaming?
God in flesh to dwell
The shepherds praising
Good news, joyous Noel
Others will be seeking
His grace not withheld
I'm overwhelmed

It was the LORD Himself

BEING BORN AGAIN

Turn Around

(Adapted from the melody of "Calm Down" by Rema & Selena Gomez)

God turned His back on Jesus	Rom 5:8
We're all hell bound	
Submit yourself to be found, to be found, to be found	Rom 6:23
Then God will turn around	
He'll turn around, He'll turn around	Gen 32:30
And receive you like His own Son, His own Son	Eph 1:3–6

All of this is so beautiful	Eccl 3:11
You can feel it in your soul	Ps 62:1
You're His beloved	Jer 31:3
It's irrefutable	
He's invisible	John 5:37

If you want to lay down and rest in green meadows	Ps 23:2
You have to enter through the correct gate that is narrow	Matt 7:13–14
If you want to have prosperity that is bestowed	2 Cor 9:8
Your life must change like Saul on the Damascus Road	Acts 9

You have to be transformed	Rom 12:2
You need to be informed	Prov 22:17
You must work in unison	Col 3:13–15
You'll be embraced	Luke 15:20
He'll surround you with warmth	1 John 3:1; Jas 2:16
You'll be safe and secure	Ps 91:4
Quiet yourself and carefully listen	Ps 46:10; Rom 10:17
The Holy Spirit will whisper	John 16:13; 1 Kgs 19:11–13

When you sin, you turn your back: renounce	Acts 3:19
But God loves you despite, His grace super abounds	Rom 5:20
Then if you want to make it right	Rom 3:21–31
Interact if you want to reunite	2 Cor 5:18
All this to your heart's delight	Ps 37:4

God turned His back on Jesus
We're all hell bound
Submit yourself to be found, to be found, to be found
Then God will turn around, He'll turn around, He'll turn around
And receive you like His own Son, His own Son

All of this is so beautiful
You can feel it in your soul
You're His beloved
It's irrefutable; He's invisible

His agape love is the secret ingredient	John 3:16; 1 Cor 13
When God touches your heart, it's immediate	1 John 3:14
You'll respond with true obedience	John 14:15–17
You'll always remember this experience	2 Pet 3:15–16

When He turns around	
You will see His face	Ezek 39:29; Gen 32:30
He'll call your name and you'll be ordained	John 15:14–16
You will forever be without blame	Phil 2:15–18
Beside Him, you'll reign	2 Tim 2:12; Rev 3:21

God turned His back on Jesus
We're all hell bound
Submit yourself to be found, to be found, to be found
Then God will turn around, He'll turn around, He'll turn around
And receive you like His own Son, His own Son

All of this is so beautiful
You can feel it in your soul
You're His beloved
It's irrefutable; He's invisible

Saved, Loved, Blessed, and Approved

(Adapted from the melody of "That I Would Be Good"
by Alanis Morissette)

That I would be saved even though I am human	2 Cor 5:21
That I would be saved	
Even if I failed to obey	Eph 2:5; Rom 5:1–21
That I would be saved if I had a bad day	Isa 41:10
That I would be saved even if I lost my way	Luke 15:1–7
That I would be loved even if I turned my back	Jer 15:19
That I would be loved even if I didn't love myself	Rom 5:8
That I would be loved	
If I didn't behave my best this time	1 Tim 1:15
That I would be loved if I were not all caring	Col 1:21–22
That I would be blessed even when I hurt myself	Gal 5:14
That I would be blessed	
Even when I do not deserve this	1 John 4:18
That I would be blessed even when I was upset	Job 21
That I would be blessed even if I felt dirty	1 John 3:1
That I would be approved even if I missed the boat	2 Cor 5:9–11
That I would be approved 'cause You chose me	
And I received	Eph 1:4–5

The River

Feeling the sun warming our souls
Floating in water, then sinking below
Soaking our bodies deep in the flood
Then rising to surface freed from the mud

Drifting along the riverbank
Watching the rocks pass below the plank
As splashes of water onto our faces
Fall from high above, sprinkling with grace

A fish swims by, a frog boasts a croak
And above in the cliffs where a fire smokes
An eagle flies by with a mouse in grip
As its young's calls echo through the forest crypt

A log sits afloat, the rapids race by
While hauling the debris cradled in the tide
The trees sway forth where they dance in the wind
While the clouds in the sky are tracing the brim

And on the beach, the sand burns hot
A crab pounces out from behind a rock
It springs on a bug to devour it whole
As a crow caws loudly, it's hunger shows

An empty canoe painted with aged wood
Is tied to a dock, returned there for good
The deer dash away while none have stayed
They drank from the river as our approach was made

The path turns left, the sun disappears
It's shaded by the wall of sandstone that nears
The speed picks up, the banks go blur
The valley is revealed as the river turns

The wind picks up, and the tide crashes in
The river, now a lake, wears an unfamiliar grin
The raft spins round, the sky above tunnels
The raft slows down, beneath the water bubbles

We're pulled to a stream surrounded by a cave
The calmness sleeps upon its grave
The heat is lost, and the walls are seared
As we drift with death, the darkness is feared

Our hearts pound fast, and our echoes screech
The raft floats forth tightly clamping its teeth
The water runs quiet, the stillness grips
And in the cavern down, water trickling drips

The cave will forbid what the river shall forgive   Mark 16:16
And the raft will devour what the water
    shall empower   Eph 4:4–6; Rom 6:3–4
The cave will forbid what the river shall forgive
And the raft will devour what the water shall empower

A light forms near, we all breath at ease
There is an escape sensed beyond what is seen

    1 Cor 10:13

We come out alive, our souls gasp relief
Then the raft hits sand as we cast our grief   1 Pet 5:7

The sand is warm and the sun's light's on our face
As His blood we drink, and His body we taste   John 6:53–57
Our raft is left behind as we walk
It has served its purpose: His Word was taught   Rom 8:28

The cave will forbid what the river shall forgive
And the raft will devour what the water shall empower
The cave will forbid what the river shall forgive
And the raft will devour what the water shall empower

Then later that day as more stumble by
They find the raft, they board in no time
Then off they go to follow the tide
With their faith in hand, and again He guides

Ps 37:23–24; Prov 16:9

Thus, feeling the sun warming our souls
Floating in water, then sinking below
Soaking our bodies deep in the flood
Then rising to surface freed from the mud . . .

The cave will forbid what the river shall forgive
And the raft will devour what the water shall empower
The cave will forbid what the river shall forgive
And the raft will devour what the water shall empower

Bearing Fruit

The life of a Christian
Some say imitates that of a plant   Ps 1:3
Want to know more? May I expound?

It starts with a pot of dirt
and God supplies the seed that   2 Cor 9:10
He Himself carefully pushes down
Covers, then pats around

Like a new birth made human   John 3:3–7
Out of nothing that becomes your life—and that's proven
                                                             Gen 2:7

Forget what's lost
One conclusion
Accept the cost

A seedling only develops out from a sprout
Your life without God soon becomes a drought   Eccl 1:14
With loving care
The plant grows in size, matures
                                          Isa 64:8; Col 1:28–29
Eventually it bears fruit, and it endures   John 15:5–8
Then savored   Eph 2:8–10

God is the sunshine that we need   1 John 1:5
His word the water   John 7:37–39
Our time with Him develops ourselves   2 Cor 3:18
Daily prayer each and every day   1 Thess 5:16–18
supplies us energy   Philippians 4:19
To be a blessing for others   Prov 11:25; John 15:12
As we cover and pat around

Like a new birth made human
Out of nothing that becomes your life—and that's proven
Forget what's lost
One conclusion
Accept the cost

A seedling only develops out from a sprout
Your life without God soon becomes a drought
With loving care, the plant grows in size, matures
Eventually it bears fruit, and it endures

A seedling only develops out from a sprout
Your life without God soon becomes a drought
With loving care, the plant grows in size, matures
Eventually it bears fruit, and it endures
Then savored, then it's savored
Yes, then it's savored

Has Your Name Been Changed by God?

(Adapted from the melody of "Lie" by NF)

Your name has some kind of meaning
Of which God has designed it like   Isa 43:1
And when you become a new creation
He changes your name to ripe   Rev 2:17
Its final meaning altered just to match your life   John 10:2–4
And now you got to be like that
You've got a divine contract   Rom 8:29–30

Yeah, the first person to have their name changed was Abram
Which means "exalted father."
God inserted His grace into Abram's being   Gen 17:4–6
He became Abraham, "the father of many nations"
Abraham's wife Sarai means "contentious or quarrelsome"
Again, God shared His grace adding it to her name
Sarah, which means "princess"   Gen 17:15–16

And in their old age after their names were changed
God blessed them with a baby
His name was Isaac which means "laughter"   Gen 17:19
"Everyone who hears about this will laugh with me"   Gen 17:17
And then there was Jacob which means "cheater or deceiver"
He had his named changed to Israel
Which means "God's people"   Gen 35:10–11
As a prince, He has power with God and with men
And he has prevailed
Then Nebuchadnezzar changed the name
Of Mattaniah to Zedekiah   2 Kgs 24:17
From "Gift of YAHWEH" to "the Lord is righteous"
Making him king in his place

Your name has some kind of meaning
of which God has designed it like
And when you become a new creation,
He changes your name to ripe
Its final meaning altered just to match your life
And now you got to be like that, you've got a divine contract

Look, the king ordered the chief eunuch
To change the names of four people   Dan 1:7
He gave the name Belteshazzar to Daniel
From "God is judge" to "the chief deity of Babylon"
Shadrach to Hananiah, from "gift of the lord"
To "the command of Aku, the moon God"
Meshach to Mishael
From "who is what God is" to "who is as Aku"
And Abednego to Azariah
From "whom Jehovah helps" to "the God of science and literature"

Then Moses changed the name Hosea to Joshua   Num 13:16
From "salvation" to "Jehovah saves"
Pharaoh changed the name
Of Joseph to Zaphenath-Paneah   Gen 41:45
From "may Jehovah give increase" to "God speaks"
Jesus renamed Simon to Peter from "listen" to "rock"   John 1:42
And finally, from Hebrew to Latin or Greek,
Saul's name became Paul   Acts 13:9
From "prayed for" to "little or small"

Your name has some kind of meaning
Of which God has designed it like
And when you become a new creation,
He changes your name to ripe
Its final meaning altered just to match your life
And now you got to be like that, you've got a divine contract

Which do you prefer? Your former name or your new one?
Speak up, which do you prefer? There's something in store for you
When God changes your name, its purpose is significant
Indeed, which do you prefer? Your new one!

Your name has some kind of meaning
Of which God has designed it like
And when you become a new creation
He changes your name to ripe
Its final meaning altered just to match your life
And now you got to be like that, you've got a divine contract

Has your name been changed by God?
Has your name been changed by God?

You now have a new identity

Saved Man

(Adapted from the melody of "Spaceman" by Nick Jonas)

People are too easily offended	Matt 24:10, 12
Many feel like they're resented	
But I feel like a saved man	
I know I'm a saved man	1 John 5:13

Too many of us teeter on the brink
In a few more years, we'll be extinct
But I feel like a saved man
I know I'm a saved man

Confess with your mouth	
"Jesus is Lord" just to quote	Rom 10:9–11
And "believe in your heart that God raised Him" as it's wrote	
You're a saved man	
Yeah, you're a saved man	

Jesus dying on the cross for us is profound	John 3:17
The awareness that we're worthy of this should astound	
	Ps 111:2–7
I'm a saved man	
Yeah, I'm a saved man	

A new creature—redo	2 Cor 5:17
Old things pass away	
Then become new	1 John 2:17; Matt 24:35; Rev 21
For a reason unknown, I'm a saved man	Col 1:16
Yeah, yeah, I'm a saved man	

If not, then the rest of you are doomed	Isa 1:4–14
To be thrown into the Lake of Fire and marooned	Rev 20:15
I'm never alone, I'm a saved man	Isa 41:10
Yeah, yeah, I'm a saved man	

Reap what you sow . . .   Gal 6:7–8
Blessed are those who don't see, no proof   John 20:29
And yet believe on their own
You're called to be a saved man   Rom 1:6
Know that you're a saved man

I'm born again, now awoke
A future and so much hope   John 3:11
I'm definitely a saved man, I know I'm a saved man

A new creature—redo
Old things pass away, then become new
I'm never alone, I'm a saved man
Yeah, yeah, I'm a saved man

If not, then the rest of you are doomed
To be thrown into the Lake of Fire and marooned
I don't wanna roam, I'm a saved man
Yeah, yeah, I'm a saved man

Reap what you sow . . .
Blessed are those who don't see, no proof
And yet believe on their own
He has a master plan   Jer 29:11; Prov 3:5–6; John 1:11–13
Know that you're a saved man

A new creature—redo
Old things pass away, then become new
I'm never alone, I'm a saved man
Yeah, yeah, I'm a saved man

If not, then the rest of you are doomed
To be thrown into the Lake of Fire and marooned
I don't wanna roam, I'm a saved man
Yeah, yeah, I'm a saved man

Reap what you sow . . .
And never be alone
Do you wanna see?
Defeat a thousand men with a jawbone   Judg 15:19
And never be alone
Do you wanna see?
Defeat a thousand men with a jawbone
I'm a saved man
(Ooh, ooh, I'm a saved man)

Small Town U.S.A.

(Adapted from the melody of "Die For You" by The Weeknd)

From a very early age, my mom died; and I had to make do
This is what altered my life's view; and I thank You

The process during was difficult as I saw things unfold
In hindsight, it made me more bold
This despite my youth   Heb 4:16
It's true, which path would I choose?

I was badly broken, a blessing in disguise
I returned to my faith, once again baptized   Acts 2:38
I found my true purpose, my emotional pain defined
My future's wide open, how high would I climb?

No more concealing, I'm one of His beloved   3 John 1:2
At the point of depletion, forgiven by His blood   Eph 1:7
Just like He was resurrected
I'm not afraid to admit it   Luke 24:6–7
How much my childhood played

Growing up so stable—who knew it?
Her death became my milestone
I grew up in Peru; it's true, I grew up in Peru
His perfect strength shines through my weakness
If God and I remain aligned   2 Cor 12
I grew up in Peru; it's true, I grew up in Peru

I grew up poor and played sports and just didn't think things
    through
My best friends were everything, the glue; and together, we grew
Riding bikes was so much pleasure
Always outside regardless of the weather
The things we used to do, innocence in review

I was an altar boy, to no one's surprise
Your name was known to all; so grateful, I recognize   Heb 8:10
What I'm learning is
God protects us if you confirm Him   2 Thess 3:3
I carry this today

Growing up so stable—who knew it?
Her death became my milestone
I grew up in Peru; it's true, I grew up in Peru
His perfect strength shines through my weakness if God
And I remain aligned
I grew up in Peru; it's true, I grew up in Peru

I grew up in Peru, can't wait to return to
It's like a tattoo, forever with you
And surely, I'll keep praying   1 Thess 5:16–17
I grew up in Peru, can't wait to return to
It's like a tattoo, forever with you
And surely, I'll keep praying

Growing up so stable—who knew it?
Her death became my milestone
I grew up in Peru; it's true, I grew up in Peru
His perfect strength shines through my weakness if God
And I remain aligned
I grew up in Peru; it's true, I grew up in Peru

Planted Seed

(Adapted from the melody of "Sunroof" by Nicky Youre & dazy)

I used to need some kind of real proof   John 20:27
But today I can safely assume
And deep inside my heart, You have replied

I always prayed to learn the truth   1 Thess 5:16–17; Ps 86:11
Now, I seem to have a clue
And because of You, I now grow so wise   1 Cor 4:10

It all started with a man named Aaron, who had wit
We connected at work, then later I'd permit
Awkward at first when we'd pray in the open and on-the-spot
He planted a seed which grew   Mark 4

Yeah, he would work on my unit at night
A veil was lifted, and I was no longer blind   2 Cor 3:16
I'm grateful for his debut

I resigned that my life was no longer mine   1 Cor 6:19–20
Review, renew, brand new   2 Cor 5:17

I used to need some kind of real proof
But today I can safely assume
And deep inside my heart, You have replied

I always prayed to learn the truth
Now, I seem to have a clue
And because of You, I now grow so wise

I used to need some kind of real proof . . .
I always prayed to learn the truth . . .

LET ME SAVE YOU

Yeah, he would work on my unit at night
A veil was lifted, and I was no longer blind
I'm grateful for his debut

I resigned that my life was no longer mine
Review, renew, brand new

I used to need some kind of real proof
But today I can safely assume
And deep inside my heart, You have replied

I always prayed to learn the truth
Now, I seem to have a clue
And because of You, I now grow so wise

It Just Came Out of the Blue

(Adapted from the melody of "Fire For You" by Cannons)

It just came out of the blue	
Immersed in glow	2 Cor 4:6
Then forgiveness ensued	Eph 1:7
Out from the shadows	1 Pet 2:9

How quickly my spirit grew	2 Pet 3:18
My flesh abruptly exposed	2 Tim 2:22
A new beginning debuted; my nature's subdued	2 Cor 5:17
And I want to say thank you	Isa 12:4–5

I've been adopted	Eph 1:5; Gal 4:4–5
I have so much more to do	1 Cor 7:17
And my response:	
Money's not my revenue	1 Tim 6:10; Matt 6:19–21

It just came out of the blue, it just came out of the blue

It just came out of the blue	
Your loveliness surrounds	Ps 33:22; Ps 23:6
You work through me in lieu	Eph 2:10
This agreement astounds	Ps 111:2–7

I know You will see it through from above	Ps 115:1–3
You give me my voice	Isa 51:16; Jer 1:9
I know You live inside	
To change me into Christ's image to	2 Cor 3:18; Rom 8:29
Help anyone who needs You	Rom 10:13–15

I've been adopted
I have so much more to do
And my response:
Money's not my revenue

LET ME SAVE YOU

I've been adopted
I have so much more to do
And my response:
Money's not my revenue

It just came out of the blue, it just came out of the blue

Born Again

(Adapted from the melody of "When I'm Gone" by Alesso & Katy Perry)

"In the spirit, you have to be born again	John 3:5–7
To enter into My Kingdom	
From the water, Amen," He says	Matt 3:16

"In the spirit, you have to be born again	
To enter into My Kingdom"	
Nor did He gripe the required stripes	Isa 53:5

He gave His life freely, freely to save me	John 10:18; John 10:11
And then to embrace me	Jer 31:3

He provides me with plenty	Phil 4:19
He gave up everything	Heb 9:28
Just to redeem me	1 Cor 28–31; Gal 3:13–14

He recites lovingly, lovingly	1 John 4:9–10
That in three days He arose	Matt 28:5–6; 1 Cor 15:3–4

He calls me by my name	
Imploring me, imploring me	John 10:1–21
To question the status quo	Matt 21:12–13

"In the spirit, you have to be born again
To enter into My Kingdom
From the water, Amen," He says

"In the spirit, you have to be born again
To enter into My Kingdom"
Nor did He gripe the required stripes

Repent: change your views
A creature becomes brand new   2 Cor 5:17
Then, you'll never regret   Isa 40:31; Phil 3:12–14

"In the spirit, you have to be born again
To enter into My Kingdom"
Nor did He gripe the required stripes

He was born in a manger, He sacrificed greater   Luke 2:6–7
To become our sustainer   Isa 46:4
Death—many try to explain it
Many try to escape it   Eccl 8:8; Heb 9:27
Many try to recreate it   Gal 6:7–8; Rev 9:6; Rom 8:5

He recites lovingly, lovingly
That in three days He arose

Well, let's suppose: A prophecy? A philosophy?   2 Pet 1:20
But what happens if it comes tomorrow?   Matt 24:35–37

"In the spirit, you have to be born again
To enter into My Kingdom
From the water, Amen," He says

"In the spirit, you have to be born again
To enter into My Kingdom"
Nor did He gripe the required stripes

Repent: change your views, a creature becomes brand new
Then, you'll never regret

"In the spirit, you have to be born again
To enter into My Kingdom"
Nor did He gripe the required stripes

In the spirit, in the spirit

About the Author

Eric Zack is a born-again Christian who resorted to poetry as his preferred emotional outlet at the age of twenty years old. At that time, his dear mother died from metastatic cancer at the age of thirty-nine years old. His mother's cancer was not directly talked about in the open with him or his three younger brothers, although she was diagnosed several years before her death. He was raised in a stable middle-class home environment in a small town in the middle of the United States in the Roman Catholic faith and served as an altar boy for several years growing up. He had a difficult time processing what had happened and stepped away from his faith temporarily as he coped and adjusted with this "new normal." Fortunately, he soon returned to his faith with a renewed passion to develop a closer relationship with his Savior Jesus Christ while trying to better understand life, suffering, loss, and healing. His personal mission statement and professional goals have been to "make a difference and help others" because he was not able to do so for his mother.

Since a young age, Eric has generally possessed an introvert personality type and has often kept his thoughts and feelings private for the most part until now. He is also an experienced and expert oncology nurse and nursing college professor in response to his mom's death, which occurred during his third year of college. Today, he is married and has four adult children, none of whom have ever met his mother. Eric's poetry has dealt with most aspects of living life and covers many different, unique topics that most human beings will experience. More recently, he has been driven to write about many aspects of his maturing Christian faith. He noted a significant gap in the literature in regard to Christian poetry that is supported by the Holy Bible and the many truths that the Holy Bible shares. As a result, he wanted to publish his poetry collections to share with whomever is interested in learning more about these topics, whomever enjoys reading and meditating on various Bible verses, and whomever enjoys poetry in general. He felt it a priority at this time in his life to pursue publishing these five volumes to help others in their spiritual journeys given today's serious crises and waning timeline.

His other poetry collections that are not directly related to Christianity may be published at a future date. Eric's poetry style is typically rhythmic and rhyming in nature with repeated chorus lines (almost like a song) to support certain important aspects worth stressing. Up to this point, his poems have been hidden from all and considered amateur (never shared or published before). This has been his "quiet" passion for over thirty years now; and he hopes that some good may come out of him sharing these authentic, cherished poems that are very personal and private in nature. He sincerely believes that the Holy Spirit has coauthored most of these, using him as a vessel to reach others who are in desperate need of answers and/or support.

Thank you for allowing small pieces of me and my life's insight into your reality and life. And may Jesus Christ have all the power, praise, and glory for doing so. And may God continue to bless you and your loved ones as you seek to get closer and closer to Him. In Christ Jesus, Eric.

Printed in the USA
CPSIA information can be obtained
at www.ICGtesting.com
LVHW051932091224
798519LV00004B/18